DISCARD

Bicycle Science Projects

Other titles in the *Science Fair Success* series

Science Fair Success

Bicycle Science Projects

Physics on Wheels

Robert Gardner

Enslow Publishers, Inc.

40 Industrial Road   PO Box 38
Box 398   Aldershot
Berkeley Heights, NJ 07922 Hants GU12 6BP
USA   UK

http://www.enslow.com

Library of Congress Cataloging-in-Publication Data

Gardner, Robert, 1929–
     Bicycle science projects : physics on wheels / Robert Gardner.
        v. cm. — (Science fair success)
     Includes bibliographical references and index.
     Contents: The emergence of bicycles — Bikes, gears, and speed — Using your
bicycle to measure distance and speed — Forces every cyclist must overcome or apply.
     ISBN 0-7660-1630-7 (hardcover)
     1. Force and energy—Experiments—Juvenile literature. 2. Speed—Experiments—
Juvenile literature. 3. Bicycles—Experiments—Juvenile literature. [1. Bicycles and
bicycling. 2. Bicycles and bicycling—Experiments. 3. Experiments. 4. Science projects.]
I. Title. II. Series.
QC73.4.G37 2004
531'.6
                                     2003026961
Printed in the United States of America

10 9 8 7 6 5 4 3 2 1

To Our Readers:
We have done our best to make sure all Internet Addresses in this book were active and
appropriate when we went to press. However, the author and the publisher have no control over
and assume no liability for the material available on those Internet sites or on other Web sites they
may link to. Any comments or suggestions can be sent by e-mail to comments@enslow.com or to
the address on the back cover.

Illustration Credits: Tom LaBaff

Photo Credits: Getty Images, p. 14; Library of Congress, p. 19; Photo Courtesy of Just
Two Bikes, Manufacturer, and James M. Muellner, Designer, p. 24.

Cover Photo: © Tim Davis/Photo Researchers, Inc.

Contents

Introduction

You may be surprised to learn that more bicycles than automobiles are sold each year. Because bicycles are so common, it is likely that either you or someone in your family owns one. Assuming you can ride a two-wheeler, there are a lot of experiments you can do with a bike. And, since riding a bike is fun, you can have fun and learn a lot of science as well.

This book provides many experiments you can do with your bicycle. In general, the easier experiments are found in the early chapters. The more challenging experiments are in the last two chapters. But do not stop experimenting after you finish reading this book. As you do experiments, you will probably think of other experiments of your own. That is the way science works: one experiment leads to another.

As you experiment with your bicycle, keep a notebook handy. If possible, buy a notebook that has graph paper on at least some pages so that you can make graphs and diagrams easily. Jot down your ideas, data, and observations in your notebook. When you do experiments, explain what you are doing and record the measurements, numbers, and other factual information you collect.

Often the solution to a difficult problem or the beginning of a new idea arises unexpectedly. It may happen when you are relaxing, sleeping, dreaming, awakening, or, like me, when you are riding your bike. That is why many scientists keep one small notebook beside their bed and one in their pocket. They

Bicycle Science Projects

record their thoughts when ideas come to mind. They know that if they don't, they are likely to forget them.

When you use a bicycle for experiments, you will have to take measurements and do calculations. So, you will find a calculator a handy tool. Perhaps you can keep one, along with your notebook and a pencil, in a carrying bag fastened to your bike.

Science Fairs

Judges at science fairs do not reward projects or experiments that are simply copied from a book. For example, a diagram or model of a bicycle would not impress most judges; however, a unique method for measuring acceleration while riding your bicycle would attract their attention.

Science fair judges tend to reward creative thought and imagination. It is difficult to be creative or imaginative unless you are really interested in your project. Be sure to choose a subject that appeals to you. And before you jump into a project, consider, too, your own talents and the cost of materials you will need.

If you decide to use an experiment found in this book for a science fair, you should find ways to modify or extend it. This should not be difficult because you will discover that as you do these projects, new ideas for experiments will come to mind—experiments that could make excellent science fair projects, particularly because the ideas are your own and are interesting to you. Some ideas for such projects can be found at the end of some experiments in this book.

If you decide to enter a science fair and have never done so before, you should read some of the books listed in the Further Reading section. These books deal specifically with science fairs and will provide plenty of helpful hints and lots of useful information that will enable you to avoid the pitfalls that sometimes plague first-time entrants. You will learn how to prepare appealing reports that include charts and graphs, how to set up and display your work, how to present your project, and how to talk to judges and visitors.

Safety First

Most of the projects included in this book are perfectly safe. **If any danger is involved in doing an experiment, it will be made known to you. In some cases, to avoid any danger to you, you will be asked to work with an adult. Please do so.** We do not want you to take any chances that could lead to an injury. The following safety rules are well worth reading before you start any project.

1. Whenever doing experiments that involve riding a bicycle, you should **wear an approved helmet and close-toed shoes.**

2. Do any experiments or projects, whether from this book or of your own design, under the supervision of a science teacher or other knowledgeable adult.

3. Read all instructions carefully before proceeding with a project. If you have questions, check with your supervisor before going any further.

4. Maintain a serious attitude while conducting experiments. Fooling around can be dangerous to you and to others.

5. Wear approved safety goggles when you are working with anything that might cause injury to your eyes.

6. Do not eat or drink while experimenting.

7. Have a first-aid kit nearby while you are experimenting.

8. Do not place your fingers too close to the spokes of a rapidly spinning bicycle wheel.

Metric Measurements

In science, most measurements are made in metric units such as meters, kilograms, newtons, and joules. However, you may find it easier to locate a yardstick than a meterstick, and the spring scales you use may measure ounces or pounds instead of newtons. Unfortunately, calculations using feet, pounds, and foot-pounds are often difficult to understand. If you measure in U.S. conventional units, you can easily convert them to metric units using a calculator. Table 1 provides all the conversions you will need to do the experiments in this book.

Table 1: Abbreviations, in parentheses, and conversions of U.S. conventional units to metric units.

Length or Distance	Mass and Weight
1 inch (in) = 2.54 centimeters (cm)	1 pound (lb) of mass = 0.45 kilogram (kg)
1 foot (ft) = 0.3048 m	1 pound (lb) of force = 4.45 newtons (N)
1 yard (yd) = 0.9144 meter (m)	1 ounce (oz) of mass = 0.028 kilogram (kg)
1 mile (mi) = 11.61 kilometers (km)	1 ounce (oz) of force = 0.28 newton (N)
1 centimeter (cm) = 0.394 inch (in)	2.2 kilograms (kg) of mass = 1 pound (lb) of mass
1 meter (m) = 3.28 feet (ft)	4.45 newtons (N) = 1 pound (lb) of force
1 meter (m) = 1.09 yards (yd)	**Time**
1 kilometer (km) =1,000 meters (m)	1 hour (h) = 60 minutes (min) = 3,600 seconds (s)
1 meter (m) = 100 centimeters (cm)	1 second = 1/60 minute = 1/3,600 hour

Work or Energy

1 joule (J) = 1 newton-meter (N-m) = 0.74 foot-pounds (ft-lb)

Power

1 watt (W) = 1 joule/second (J/s) = 0.74 foot-pounds/second (ft-lb/s)

1 horsepower = 746 joules/second (J/s) = 550 foot-pounds/second (ft-lb/s)

Chapter 1

The Emergence of Bicycles

Americans celebrate the signing of the Declaration of Independence on July 4. The patriots in the Continental Congress who wrote and signed that document in Philadelphia may have arrived in that city on foot, on horseback, or in a horse-drawn coach. None of them pedaled to Philadelphia on a bicycle. In 1776, when that Congress was in session, there were no bicycles in colonial America or anywhere else in the world.

Bicycle History

The first bicycle, if you could call it that, appeared in France in 1791. It was called a *celerifere*, which means "fast feet." It had no gears, chain, or pedals, and there was no way to steer it. It was basically a means of remaining seated while walking in a straight line.

By 1817, Baron Karl von Drais of Karlsruhe, Germany, had significantly improved the *celerifere*. His vehicles became known as hobby horses, dandy horses, velocipedes, or

Draisiennes after their inventor. As you can see from Figure 1, these early velocipedes were steerable two-wheeled vehicles that allowed the "rider" to sit as he walked or ran. There were no pedals. Hobby horses, which were made entirely of wood, were also known as bone shakers. Even after wheelwrights learned how to make metal tires, a velocipede ride along the cobblestone streets of that era was still a bone-shaking experience.

Von Drais, who obtained a patent for his vehicle, was probably surprised to find that on downhill slopes he could raise his feet and coast along without toppling over. Before Von Drais started coasting down hills on his velocipede, no one believed a person could balance his or her body on a

Figure 1. The hobby horse, or bone shaker, was the world's first steerable bicycle. There were no pedals.

two-wheeled vehicle. Those who rode these bone shakers found that speed was the key to balancing on a two-wheeler. While it was difficult to balance on a velocipede at rest, it was easy to stay upright once the vehicle was moving along at a good speed. That may have been the hardest lesson to master when learning to ride a bicycle.

Experiment 1

Staying Upright on a Bike

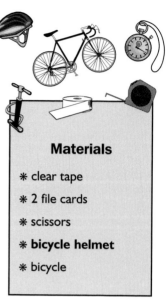

Materials

* clear tape
* 2 file cards
* scissors
* **bicycle helmet**
* bicycle

You probably rode a tricycle before you rode a bicycle. To see why, you can make simple models of a bicycle and a tricycle. Tape two file cards together as shown in Figure 2a. With a pair of scissors, make the cuts shown in Figure 2b. The cards in this form represent a bicycle because there are only two points that touch the ground. Try to make the cards stay upright (balance) on a table or floor. Not easy, is it?

Next, bend the cards outward at one end as shown in Figure 2c. You now have a simple model of a tricycle. It has three points of support. Again, place the cards on a table or floor. Notice how much easier it is to keep the cards upright when there are three points of support.

Unlike a tricycle, a bicycle has only two points of support. You can prove to yourself that it is easier to balance on a bicycle when it is moving than when it is at rest. Try to stay upright (balanced) on a bicycle that is not moving. Then see how much easier it is to maintain your balance on a bicycle when it is moving. Is it easier to balance when you ride slowly or fast? Why do you think it is so much easier to maintain your balance on a moving bicycle?

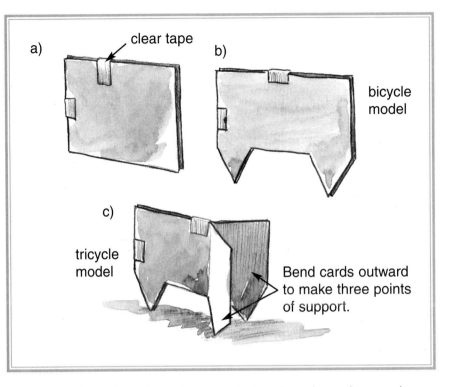

Figure 2. A simple model of a bicycle and a tricycle can be used to see why it is so much easier to ride a tricycle.

More Bicycle History

Not only could a rider stay upright while coasting on a velocipede, he could also beat horse-drawn wagons over a two-hour race. A velocipedist could go downhill much faster than a horse and wagon. Riding a hobby horse in the early nineteenth century, though very uncomfortable, was a faster means of transportation than walking or riding in a horse-drawn wagon.

The next stage in the evolution of the bicycle occurred in 1839. Having discovered that it was possible to keep one's body balanced on a moving two-wheeled vehicle, a Scottish blacksmith named Kirkpatrick Macmillan added pedals with rods connecting them to the rear wheel. Velocipede riders could now say, "Look, Mom, no feet on the ground!"

The next major step took place in Paris in 1861. To reduce all the complicated levers in Macmillan's machine, Pierre Michaux made a velocipede that had the pedals attached to the hub of the *front* wheel. Michaux's invention was simple and resembled present-day tricycles except that it had only one wheel in back. His machine was uncomplicated and easy to ride, but it was slow.

To provide a faster ride, manufacturers began making the front wheel bigger. In this way, the bike would travel farther with each turn of the pedals. Long-legged riders, because they could reach the pedals on the axle of a larger front wheel, could really whiz along. These machines, the first to be called bicycles, had wheels with diameters of 1.5 meters (nearly 5 feet) or more. Known also as high-wheelers or pennyfarthings, they were the first two-wheeled vehicles to have solid rubber tires. The rubber offered a somewhat smoother ride than tires made of wood or metal.

Pennyfarthings, while popular with cyclists seeking speed, were widely cursed by farmers and people headed to town in their horse-drawn carriages or wagons. Why? Horses were frequently frightened by these high-wheeled vehicles and would bolt or rear when they saw a cyclist passing. Farmers would purposely force cyclists off the road, hinder their passing on a narrow road, or even thrust sticks through the spokes of a cyclist's front wheel and watch with delight as the rider took a disastrous spill.

High-wheelers, while faster than Michaux's velocipedes, were more dangerous. As you can see from Figure 3, the rider,

tricycle

high-wheeler

Figure 3. How would you like to ride a high-wheeler, circa 1880? If you were to ride this bicycle, how would you get started?

seated above and only slightly behind the center of the large front wheel, had a long way to fall. If the front wheel hit a rock, the rider could take a "header," his legs trapped under the handlebars. Lacking safety helmets, people died as a result of bicycle accidents.

For ladies, whose long skirts made pedaling a high-wheeler impossible, and for professional gentlemen who did not wish to risk their necks, manufacturers began making tricycles. These vehicles had two large rear wheels connected by levers to pedals on a smaller front wheel.

Tricycles became very popular among women, who were finally able to move about easily by themselves. In fact, Susan B. Anthony, who led the women's suffrage movement in America during the second half of the nineteenth century, is reported to have said, "The bicycle [tricycle] has done more for the emancipation of women than anything else in the world."

By 1885, John Starley—whose uncle, James Starley, invented the steel-spoked wheel—had designed a safer bicycle, known as the Rover. John Starley's bike was similar to modern bikes. It placed the rider nearer the ground, between two wheels connected by a sturdy triangular steel frame. Cranks turned by feet on pedals caused a front sprocket to rotate. That sprocket was connected by a chain to a smaller sprocket mounted on the rear wheel. Because the front sprocket was larger than the rear one, Starley's bicycle was capable of high speed. However, riders often had to walk up hills, pushing their bikes, or ride a weaving, back-and-forth pattern across the road to reduce the steepness of the path at the cost of pedaling farther.

Experiment 2

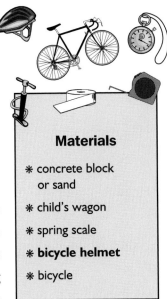

Uphill Strategy

Early cyclists often weaved back and forth across the road in order to ascend a steep hill. You can do an experiment to see why they rode this way. Place a concrete block or some sand in a child's wagon. Then, as shown in Figure 4a, use a spring scale to measure the force needed to

Materials

* concrete block or sand
* child's wagon
* spring scale
* **bicycle helmet**
* bicycle

pull the wagon straight up a steep hill. Record the force required to do this.

Next, measure the force needed to pull the wagon upward at an angle that does not point directly uphill, as shown in Figure 4b(ii). Which path requires less force? Now can you explain why early cyclists used to weave back and forth across a steep hill rather than riding straight up it?

If you have access to a wide bicycle path with a hill, you could repeat this experiment on your bicycle. (**Do not try this on a road used by cars!**) First, ride straight up the hill. Then, in the same gear, weave back and forth across the path as you ascend the hill. Which path is easier to pedal? Can you explain why?

Still More Bicycle History

In 1888, Johnny Dunlop complained to his father about the rough rides he experienced on his hard-tired bicycle. His sympathetic father, John Boyd Dunlop, an Irish surgeon, responded by inventing the pneumatic (air-filled) tire. When riders on bikes equipped with Dunlop's air-filled tires began winning all

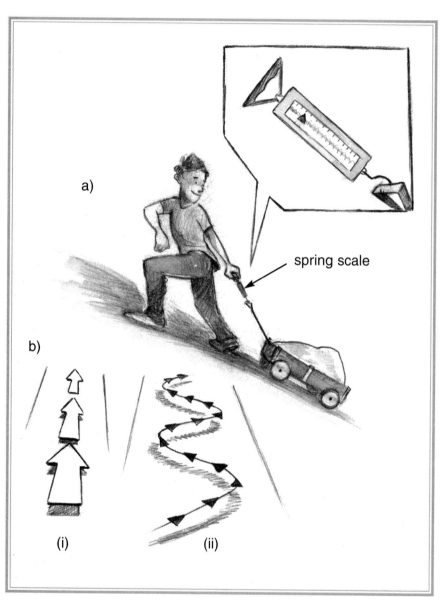

spring scale

a)

b)

(i)   (ii)

Figure 4. a) Use a spring scale to measure the force needed to pull a wagon up a steep hill. b) How does the force needed to pull the wagon straight up the hill (i) compare with the force needed along a weaving, or side-to-side, path (ii)?

the bicycle races, serious cyclists persuaded Dr. Dunlop to make more tires. Soon the Dunlop Tire Company was organized. By 1900, bikes routinely rolled on pneumatic tires mounted on wheels that turned on ball bearings. In 1899, the invention of derailleurs led to multi-geared bicycles. With the ability to change gears, bikers could pedal up hills they had previously ascended on foot or by weaving back and forth. By 1900, the bicycle was a very efficient means of transportation.

At the dawn of the twentieth century, chains had become the usual means of transferring power from the pedals to the rear wheel. However, a drive shaft, which became the way automobile engines were connected to rear wheels, was used in Pierce Arrow bicycles and other brands at about this time. During the early part of the twentieth century, the Pierce Arrow Company, using what it had learned in making bicycles, produced many very expensive and luxurious automobiles.

As the twentieth century progressed, bicycle frames became lighter and tires improved in quality and lifespan. Narrow high-pressure tires replaced the heavy balloon tires found on children's bikes in the mid-twentieth century. Improved multiple gearing made it possible to ride up hills as steep as those in the Rocky Mountains. Developments in materials engineering, brought on in part by America's space programs, led to strong yet lightweight bicycle frames made of aluminum, titanium, or carbon fiber. Separate hand brakes for rear and front wheels replaced the inefficient coaster brake.

The mountain bike, introduced in the last quarter of the twentieth century, has thick, wide tires; a strong but light frame; and 18- or 21-speed gearing designed to make it possible to ride through steep, rugged territory. Its popularity grew as city cyclists discovered that such a bike was also well suited for streets pocked by potholes and metal grates. Older bicycle enthusiasts were attracted to the mountain bike because its higher handlebars and wider seat allowed them to ride in a more comfortable upright position, reducing neck and back tension and fatigue.

Recently, the recumbent cycle (Figure 5), with its longer wheelbase and small front wheel or wheels, has attracted more cyclists. The source of its name is the position of its rider, who sits in a semi-reclined, or recumbent, position. His or her spine rests against the back of a seat. The bike, which affords greater comfort and a more efficient pedaling position, is also safer. Because the rider is closer to the ground, any fall is from a much smaller height and, therefore, is less dangerous.

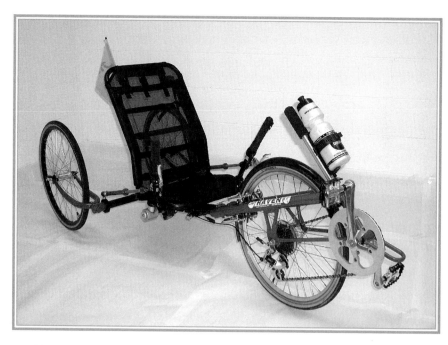

Figure 5. A rider can enjoy the comfort of a recumbent cycle. Some have two wheels; some have three.

Tandem and "Weird" Bicycles

The tandem bicycle, also known as "the bicycle built for two," became popular in the 1890s. At that time, a popular name for girls was Daisy. Daisy would, according to the old song, "look sweet upon the seat of a bicycle built for two!" These bicycles are still popular with honeymooners and parents with young children old enough to pedal. Do you think two people pedaling the single frame of a tandem bicycle can attain higher speeds than a regular one-seater?

According to *The Guinness Book of World Records,* the longest tandem bicycle ever built was one constructed by Terry Thessman in New Zealand. His bicycle was nearly 22.25 meters (73 feet) long and weighed 154 kilograms (340 pounds). As you can imagine, Thessman found he had difficulty when he came to sharp corners.

The smallest bicycle was built in 1988 by an Australian named Neville Patten. His bike had wheels that were only 1.9 cm (0.76 inch) in diameter. He managed to actually ride his bike a distance of 4.1 meters (13.5 feet). It made *The Guinness Book of World Records,* but it is not a machine that will break any sales records.

The Impact of Bicycle Technology on Automobiles and Airplanes

Few realize that the technology developed by bicycle manufacturers served as a basis for the development of automobiles and airplanes. The engineers who invented the special gears used in the tricycles that became so popular with American women led to new kinds of gears. One of these was the differential gear. This gear made it possible for two rear wheels to turn at different speeds as they went around curves. Automobiles would never have succeeded had it not been for the differential gear.

It was in their bicycle repair shop that the Wright brothers acquired the skills and learned about the materials they would need to build a vehicle that would fly. The ball bearings used to reduce friction in cars and planes were first used in bicycle wheels. The lightweight, tubular struts that made flying machines possible were devised by bicycle manufacturers. It is not unreasonable to say that the automobile and airplane industries owe a debt of gratitude to Karl von Drais, Kirkpatrick Macmillan, John Starley, and others who manufactured bicycles of ever improving efficiency.

Experiment 3

Why Wheels?

Wheels are everywhere. You can find them on cars, airplanes, trains, and roller skates, as well as on bicycles. There are wheels as large as the Ferris wheels in amusement parks and wheels as small as those in a watch. Most machines contain wheels,

Materials

* child's wagon
* sidewalk or driveway
* concrete block or another heavy object
* spring scale

though they may be hidden from view. The wheel is regarded by many as the greatest invention ever conceived by humans.

To see why wheels are so significant, try this. Take a toy wagon and turn it upside down on a sidewalk or driveway. Place a concrete block or another heavy object on the wagon as shown in Figure 6a. Notice how hard it is to pull the wagon a short distance along the surface of the walk. Then turn the wagon right-side up and place the concrete block or weight

Figure 6. An inverted wagon (a) and an upright wagon (b) can be used to show why wheels are so useful.

in the wagon (see Figure 6b). Notice how much easier it is to pull the wagon when it rolls on wheels.

If you have a spring scale, you can measure the force needed to pull the wagon when it is upside down and when it is upright and can move on wheels. How do the two forces you measured compare? Which force is greater? How many times greater?

Experiment 4

Why a Differential Gear?

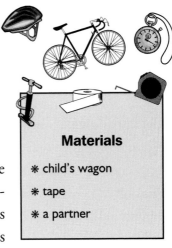

A simple experiment will convince you that development of the differential gear made automobiles possible. It allowed the drive wheels on opposite sides of the car to turn at different speeds.

Wheels on opposite sides of toy wagons are attached to a rod, the axle, that connects them. Are the rear wheels of such a wagon firmly fixed to the axle so that both wheels and the axle turn together? Or are they attached so that one wheel

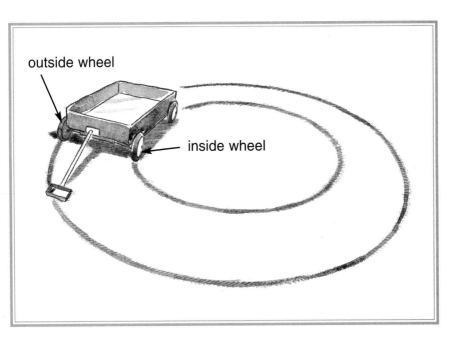

Figure 7. Pull a toy wagon along a circular path. Does an inside wheel turn the same, fewer, or more times than an outside wheel?

can turn while the other remains at rest? What about the front wheels?

Pull a toy wagon in a circle as shown in Figure 7. Does the outside wheel go around the same number of times as the inside wheel that is attached to the same axle? A piece of tape on each wheel will help you count the number of times the wheels rotate. A partner could count the turns of one wheel while you count those of the other. Does the outside wheel go around more, the same, or fewer times than the inside wheel? Can you explain why? Which wheel goes farther? Can you pull the wagon in a circle so that one wheel does not turn at all?

When an automobile goes around a curve, which drive wheel has to turn more often? What would happen if the automobile did not have a differential gear?

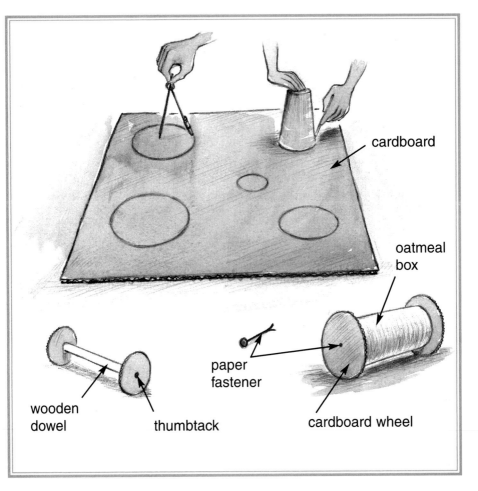

Figure 8. You can make cardboard wheels and fasten them to an "axle."

Science Project Ideas

- Use a compass (or some round objects to trace) to mark circles of various sizes, some equal, some not, on a sheet of cardboard. Use shears to cut out the circles. You now have cardboard wheels of different sizes, as shown in Figure 8. Use paper fasteners to attach the wheels firmly to opposite ends of a round box such as the kind that holds oatmeal, or thumbtack the wheels firmly to a length of wooden dowel.

  Can you make a pair of wheels that will move in a circle? Can you make a pair that will travel along a straight path?

- Do some research to find out how railroad cars go around curves.

Experiment 5

Ball Bearings, a Friction Reducer

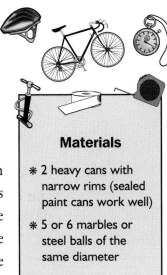

The wheels and pedal cranks on your bicycle turn on ball bearings made of steel. These bearings reduce friction and make it easier for the wheels and pedals to turn. To see how such bearings reduce friction,

Materials

* 2 heavy cans with narrow rims (sealed paint cans work well)

* 5 or 6 marbles or steel balls of the same diameter

place a heavy can, such as a one-gallon can of paint, on a similar can that has a narrow rim around its top. Try to turn the top can. Notice how difficult it is to turn the can. Next, remove the top can. Place 5 or 6 marbles or steel balls with equal diameters on the bottom can so that they can roll along the rim as shown in Figure 9. Put the second can back on top of the marbles. Try turning the upper can again. How have the "ball bearings" changed the friction between the two cans? Why do you think ball bearings are used in fast-turning wheels?

Science Project Idea

Design and carry out experiments to show ways to reduce friction without using ball bearings.

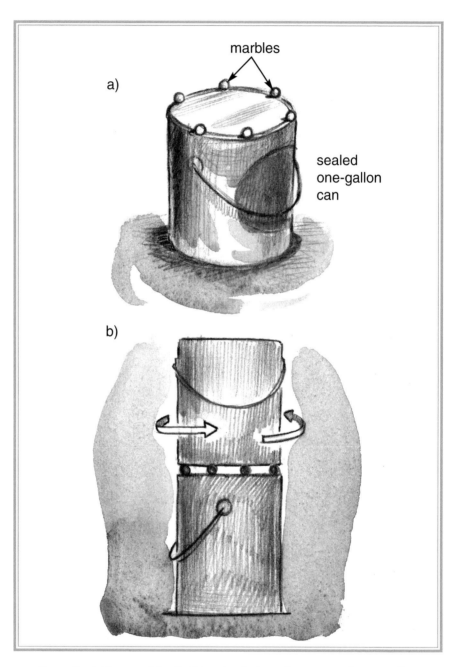

Figure 9. a) Place marbles (ball bearings) along the groove of a one-gallon can of paint. b) Place a second can on the first one. Is it easier to turn the upper can now?

Bicycles: The Forerunners of Cars, and Still a Good Way to Travel

Although transportation in America is dominated by automobiles, the bicycle is the predominant means of transportation in many Asian and African countries. Even in the United States, many people realize that their bicycles are the least expensive, and, where traffic congestion is a problem, the fastest means of going from home to work, school, or play.

Bicycles are kind to the environment. They emit none of the polluting fumes associated with cars, trucks, and buses, and they provide a healthy form of exercise for their riders. Furthermore, bicycles remain the most efficient mode of transportation known to humankind.

Chapter 2

Bikes, Gears, and Speed

If you ride a bicycle with multiple gears, you know that you use some gears to ride slowly up steep hills and other gears to move swiftly along level roads or down hills. In this chapter you will see how these gears work and why you use different combinations for different purposes.

Bicycle Gears

The pedals of your bicycle are connected to its front sprocket, as shown in Figure 10. This sprocket may consist of one, two, or three gears. The front sprocket is connected to the rear sprocket by a chain. The chain is made up of a series of links that fit over the teeth of the gears of both the front and rear sprockets. The rear sprocket usually has one, five, six, or seven gears and is part of the rear wheel. A derailleur (Figure 11) allows the chain to be shifted (moved sideways) to gears of different sizes on the rear and front sprockets, making pedaling easier or more difficult depending on the terrain. The derailleur's arm, small gears, and springs keep the chain taut despite differences in gear size.

Old bicycles had a single gear on both the front and rear sprockets. Most modern bicycles have more than one gear on both sprockets. A ten-speed bicycle has two gears on the front sprocket and five gears on the rear sprocket. Some bikes have three gears on the front sprocket and seven on the rear sprocket, so 21 different gear combinations are possible. The author's mountain bike has three gears on the front sprocket and six gears on the rear sprocket. He can ride his bike in any of 18 different gear combinations, because any one of the three front-sprocket gears can be connected to any one of the six rear-sprocket gears.

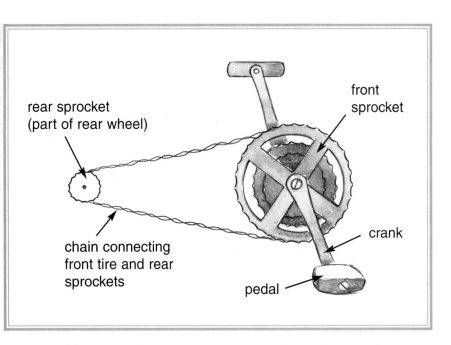

Figure 10. The pedals of a bicycle are connected to its front sprocket. A chain connects the front and rear sprockets.

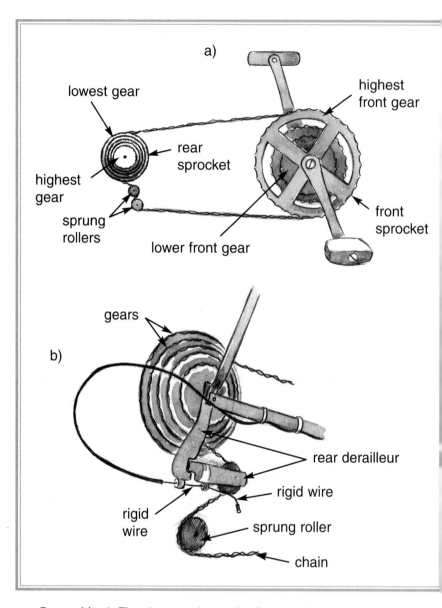

a)

lowest gear

highest front gear

rear sprocket

highest gear

sprung rollers

lower front gear

front sprocket

b)

gears

rear derailleur

rigid wire

rigid wire

sprung roller

chain

Figure 11. a) The drawing shows the front and rear sprockets with multiple gears. Derailleurs are used to move the chain inward or outward so that the rider can change from a lower to a higher gear and vice versa. b) This drawing shows a side view of a rear derailleur. Springs on the derailleur are controlled by rigid wires that are connected to shift mechanisms on the handlebars. These springs move the chain from one gear to another.

How many gears are there on the front sprocket of your bicycle? How many are on the rear sprocket? How many different gear combinations are possible on your bike? On a parent's bike? On a friend's bike?

Suppose a bicycle's chain connects a gear on the front sprocket that has 24 teeth to a gear on the rear sprocket that has 12 teeth. When the rider makes one complete turn of the pedals, the front gear goes around once because it is connected directly to the pedals. Since the gear on the rear sprocket has only 12 teeth, it must go around twice every time the front gear goes around once. Do you see why? If you don't, Experiment 6 will help you to understand.

Experiment 6

A Simple Pair of Gears

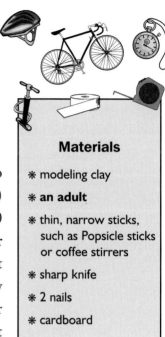

Materials

* modeling clay
* **an adult**
* thin, narrow sticks, such as Popsicle sticks or coffee stirrers
* sharp knife
* 2 nails
* cardboard

Use modeling clay to make two small disks, one about 5 cm (2 in) in diameter, and a second about 10 cm (4 in) in diameter. Then, **under adult supervision**, make 12 short "gear teeth" by cutting thin, narrow sticks, such as Popsicle sticks or coffee stirrers, into pieces about 2.5 cm (1 inch) long. Push 4 evenly spaced sticks (gear teeth) into the smaller disk and 8 evenly spaced sticks into the larger disk. Nails can be used to fasten the two gears to a small sheet of cardboard as shown in Figure 12. Place the "gears" close together so that the gear teeth mesh.

Using your hand, slowly turn the gear with 4 teeth. How many times must the gear with 4 teeth rotate for the gear with 8 teeth to make one complete turn? Next, slowly turn the gear with 8 teeth. How many times does the gear with 4 teeth rotate when you turn the gear with 8 teeth around once?

If one gear had 8 teeth and the other had 24 teeth, how many rotations would the gear with 8 teeth make when the gear with 24 teeth makes one turn? How many rotations would the gear with 24 teeth make when the gear with 8 teeth makes 6 turns?

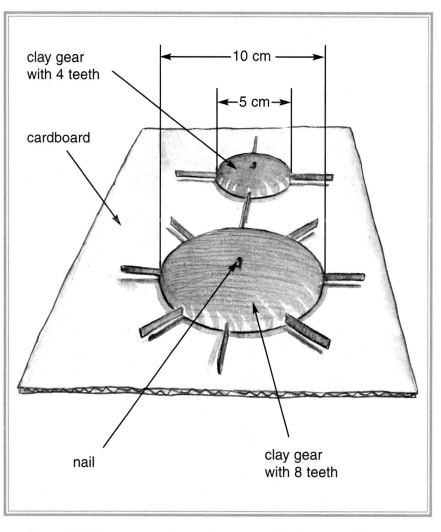

clay gear
with 4 teeth

cardboard

10 cm

5 cm

nail

clay gear
with 8 teeth

Figure 12. Make two model gears from clay and thin, short, wide sticks.
Mount the gears on cardboard with nails.

Science Project Idea

Try making gears from cardboard or Tinkertoys. Can you arrange a number of gears so that the final gear turns in the same direction (clockwise or counterclockwise) as the first one?

The Gears on Your Bicycle

Now that you understand gear connections, you can investigate the gears on your own bicycle. The steel gears on your bicycle's front and rear sprockets do not actually touch one another. Instead, they are joined by a chain. The links in the chain are made to fit perfectly over the teeth of both the front and rear gears. When you push on the bicycle's pedals and turn the front gears, the chain causes the rear gears to turn just as they would if they were meshed with the front gears.

Now let's see if you can figure out how one turn of a front-sprocket gear affects the rear-sprocket gear and the wheel to which it is firmly attached.

Experiment 7

Your Bicycle Gears

How many gears are on your bike's front sprocket (the one connected to the pedals)? How many gears are on the rear sprocket (the one connected to the rear wheel)?

Count the number of teeth on each of the gears on your front and rear sprockets. (You may want to put on a pair of old gloves before you begin to prevent your fingers from becoming greasy.) This may be done more easily if you turn the bike upside down so that it rests on its handlebars and seat. It's easy to lose count because you may not be able to see all the teeth at once. Consequently, you may want to mark one of the gear teeth with a small piece of tape or in some other way. Then you will know at which gear tooth you started your count. Record your data in a table—Table 2 is an example. The data shown in Table 2 is from the author's mountain bike. Your data may be different. You may have more or fewer gears, and the number of teeth on the gears may be different.

Materials

* bicycle, preferably one with more than one gear on both front and rear sprockets

* pair of old gloves

* marker such as a piece of tape

* pencil or pen

* paper or notebook

* a partner

* piece of chalk or a stick

* straight path such as a driveway or sidewalk

* measuring tape, meterstick, or yardstick

Table 2: Gears on front and rear sprockets and number of teeth on each gear for author's mountain bike.

Front Sprocket	Number of Teeth	Rear Sprocket	Number of Teeth
Gear 3 (biggest)	48	Gear 1 (biggest)	30
Gear 2	36	Gear 2	26
Gear 1 (smallest)	28	Gear 3	22
		Gear 4	18
		Gear 5	16
		Gear 6 (smallest)	12

Shift gears, if necessary, to connect the biggest gear on your front sprocket to the smallest gear on your rear sprocket. From the data you have collected, predict how many times the rear wheel of your bike will go around when you slowly turn the pedals through one complete rotation. You will want to hold on to the rear tire so that it does not spin freely as you turn the pedal. The final rotation of the wheel may be a fraction of a turn. How can you estimate what that fraction is?

You may find it easier and more accurate to turn the pedal around 10 times and count the number of wheel rotations. Then divide your count by 10 to estimate the number of wheel turns per pedal rotation.

If you have only one gear on both sprockets, you have completed the experiment. If you have more than one gear on either sprocket, you can repeat the experiment for some or all of the other possible gear combinations.

Which combination of gears do you think will move the bike farthest for each complete turn of the pedals? To check your prediction, put the bike in the gear combination you have predicted will move the bike the farthest. Have a partner support the bicycle while you use a piece of chalk or a stick to mark a position on a path such as a driveway or sidewalk. The mark should be on the path next to the lowest point on the bike's rear wheel, as shown in Figure 13. With your partner supporting the bike, slowly turn a pedal through one complete rotation with your hand to make the bike move slowly along the path. Then make a second mark on the path at the lowest point of the rear wheel. Use a measuring tape, meterstick, or yardstick to find out how far the bike traveled. How can you be sure that this combination is the one that will move the bike farthest for each turn of the pedals?

Which combination of gears do you think will move the bike the shortest distance for each complete turn of the pedals? To check your prediction, put the bike in the gear combination you have predicted and repeat the experiment. How can you check to be certain this gear combination moves the wheels through the shortest distance?

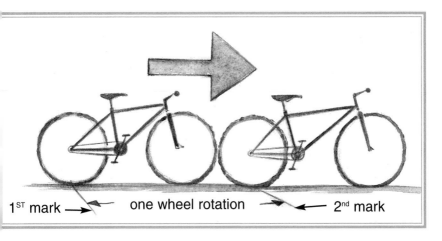

1ˢᵀ mark → one wheel rotation → ← 2ⁿᵈ mark

Figure 13. How far did the bicycle wheel go when the pedal made one complete turn?

Gears and Gear Ratios

In most automobiles with a standard-shift transmission, the driver has a choice of four or five forward gears and one reverse gear. The gears that move the car forward are called first, second, third, and so on. The gears connected to the engine, which correspond to the gears on your bicycle's front sprocket, are called the driving gears. The gears connected to the differential, which make the wheels go around, are called the driven gears. They correspond to the gears on the rear sprocket of your bicycle. When a car is in first gear, it moves at slow speeds because the number of teeth on the driving gear is small compared to the number of teeth on the driven gear. As the car is shifted into higher gears, it can move faster because the number of teeth on the driving gear compared to the number on the driven gear is made larger. As a result, the driven gear connected to the wheels goes around more often for each turn of the driving gear.

If the number of teeth on the first driving gear is 12 and the number of teeth on the driven gear is 24, we say the *ratio* of teeth on driving gear to teeth on driven gear is 12:24, or 1/2. A ratio is the quotient of one number divided by another. A ratio may be less than or greater than one. If the number of teeth on the fourth driving gear is 48 and the number of teeth on the driven gear is 24, the ratio of teeth on driving gear to driven gear is 48:24, or 2 (48/24). Thus, in first gear, the ratio of the number of teeth on the driving gear to the number on the driven gear is small. As the car is shifted from first (or low) gear, to second, to third, and finally to fourth (or high) gear, that ratio grows larger and the wheels make more turns per one turn of the driving gear.

As you have found, the gears on your bicycle work in a similar way; however, you may have more, or fewer, gears than a standard-shift car. Nevertheless, bicycles with multiple gears are still said to be in high gear when the gear with the highest number of teeth on the front sprocket is connected to the gear with the lowest number of teeth on the rear sprocket. For example, consider the bicycle in Table 2. It would be in its highest gear when gear 3 on the front sprocket is connected to gear 6 on the rear sprocket. The gear ratio would be 48:12, or 4 (48/12). The rear wheel would go around four times every time the pedals make one turn.

Gear-Inches

There is a special meaning of the word *gear* as it applies to bicycles. Cyclists often talk about gear-inches. Gear-inches are related to the distance the bicycle will travel with one turn of the pedals. It combines the gear ratio of the front and rear sprocket with the diameter of the bicycle's rear, or driving, wheel. For example, in Table 2, suppose gear 3 on the front sprocket is connected to gear 5 on the rear sprocket. The gear ratio for this connection is 3 because

$$\frac{\text{teeth on gear 3}}{\text{teeth on gear 5}} = \frac{48 \text{ teeth}}{16 \text{ teeth}} = 3$$

The rear wheel will go around three times for each rotation of the pedals.

If you multiply the gear ratio by the diameter of the wheel, you will have the gear-inches in bicycle lingo. The bicycle described in Table 2 has a wheel diameter of 26 inches. Consequently, the gear for this combination of sprocket gears in

Bicycle Science Projects

"bike-speak" is 78 gear-inches because

$$3 \text{ (the gear ratio)} \times 26 \text{ inches} = 78 \text{ gear-inches}$$

In general, the gear of a bicycle, in gear-inches, is found from the following equation:

$$\text{gear-inches} = \frac{\text{number of teeth on front sprocket gear}}{\text{number of teeth on rear sprocket gear}} \times \text{wheel diameter (in inches)}$$

Table 2 describes the gears on the front and rear sprockets of a bike. Table 3 gives the gear ratio and gear-inches for gear 3 on the front sprocket with each of the gears on the rear sprocket of the same bike.

Determine all the possible gear ratios and gear-inches for your own bicycle. Are any of the gear ratios for different gear combinations the same?

Table 3: Gear ratios and gear-inches for the bicycle described in Table 2.

Front Sprocket	Number of Teeth	Rear Sprocket	Number of Teeth	Gear Ratio	Gear-Inches
Gear 3 (biggest)	48	Gear 1 (biggest)	30	1.6	41.6
		Gear 2	26	1.85	48.0
		Gear 3	22	2.18	56.7
		Gear 4	18	2.67	69.3
		Gear 5	16	3.0	78.0
		Gear 6 (smallest)	12	4.0	104.0

A bicycle's gear, in gear-inches, is related to the distance its wheels travel with each turn of the pedals, but it is not equal to that distance. You will explore the relationship between gear-inches and the distance a bicycle travels with each turn of the pedals in Experiment 11 in the next chapter.

Science Project Idea

Determine the gear-inches for each of the gear combinations possible with your bicycle. For which gear combination is gear-inches the largest? For which combination of gears is it smallest?

Experiment 8

What Is the Actual Path of a Bicycle Wheel's Rim?

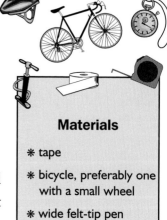

Materials

* ✳ tape
* ✳ bicycle, preferably one with a small wheel
* ✳ wide felt-tip pen
* ✳ long, wide sheet of wrapping paper
* ✳ a wall

If you watch a bicycle wheel roll along a smooth road or sidewalk, it appears to follow a circular path. But is that the path it really follows? If you were a tiny bug riding on the outside rim of a rolling wheel, would you feel as if you were on a merry-go-round? Do not forget that a wheel not only rotates, it rolls forward at the same time.

To see what this complicated motion actually looks like, put a piece of tape on the rim of a bicycle wheel. Then watch the tape as a friend slowly rolls the bike forward. Can you draw the path along which the tape moves?

You can actually map the path of a point on a rolling wheel. You can do this quite easily by firmly taping a felt-tip pen to the rim of a bicycle or tricycle wheel. (The pen must point outward.) Then roll the wheel slowly along the floor next to a long, wide sheet of wrapping paper taped to a wall so that the pen touches the paper. (Be sure the pen does not mark the wall.) The pen's wide felt tip will map the path the rim follows on the paper. How would you describe the path?

What do you predict the path followed by a point at the center of the wheel would look like? How about a point halfway between the center and the rim of the wheel?

Now, test your predictions experimentally. Were you right?

Chapter 3

Using Your Bicycle to Measure Distance and Speed

Roman soldiers used to measure distance by counting paces. A thousand paces was a mile. The Romans did not have bicycles, but we do, and you can use your bike to measure distance more accurately than the Romans did.

With the ideas developed long ago by Galileo and Newton, you can also measure the velocity of your bicycle without a speedometer. This can be done by dropping water balloons. You will also have an opportunity to confirm Galileo's discovery that objects in motion continue to move with the same speed and in the same direction unless a force (a push or a pull) acts on them.

Experiment 9

Using Your Bike to Measure Distance

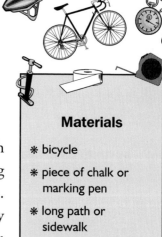

Materials

* bicycle

* piece of chalk or marking pen

* long path or sidewalk

* meterstick, yardstick, or tape measure

* piece of colored yarn

* bicycle odometer (optional)

Measuring long distances with metersticks, yardsticks, or even long tape measure can be very tedious. Your bicycle offers a much easier way to measure such lengths. All you have to do is find out how far your bike goes each time its wheels make one complete turn. After that it is a matter of counting.

If your bike has an odometer, you can use this experiment to check its accuracy. The odometer readings should give the same distances as those determined by counting the number of times your bike's front wheel goes around.

To find the distance your bicycle travels with each turn of its wheels, mark a point on the circumference of one of its tires with a piece of chalk or a marking pen. Make a similar mark on a path or sidewalk just as you did in Experiment 7 in Chapter 2 (see Figure 13). The two marks should be side by side. Now roll the bike ahead slowly until the wheel has made one complete turn and the mark is again at the bottom of the wheel. Make a second mark on the road or sidewalk. Again, the two marks should line up.

Measure the distance between the two marks on the path or sidewalk. Each turn of the wheel moves the bicycle forward a distance equal to that between the two lines you marked on the path or sidewalk. How is that distance related to the circumference of the bicycle's tire?

To make each rotation of the wheel more visible, tie a small piece of yarn to one of the spokes. How can you measure distance by counting the number of turns your bicycle wheel makes? **Do not try to ride your bike and count turns.** It is much safer to walk and push your bike when you measure distances this way!

How many times would the wheel have to rotate to measure a distance of one kilometer? To measure a distance of one mile?

Science Project Ideas

- Use your bicycle to measure some distances. You might measure the distance to your school, a store, a friend's house, a park or playground, and so on. If possible, ask a parent to measure the same distances with a car's odometer. How do your measurements compare with those made with a car? Which do you think are more accurate? What makes you think so?
- Invent other ways to measure long distances.

Experiment 10

Ratios Related to Circles

Materials

* circular objects of different size, including the wheel of a bicycle

* rulers, tape measures, or other devices to measure length

* pencil and notebook

* calculator

* geometry book or encyclopedia

Find a number of circular objects of different size, including the wheel of your bicycle. Using a ruler, tape measure, or whatever is appropriate, measure the diameter (distance across the center) and circumference (distance around the perimeter) of each of these circular objects. In some cases you may want to find the circumference in the same way you found it for your bicycle wheel in Experiment 9.

For each circular object, divide the circumference by the diameter. This will give you the ratio of the circumference to the diameter. A ratio is the quotient of one number divided by another.

How do the ratios of circumference to diameter for different circular objects compare? What can you conclude?

Consult a geometry book or encyclopedia. How do your results compare with the ratio known as pi? (The symbol for *pi* is π.) Can you explain why?

Science Project Ideas

- Find a way to measure the circumference and diameter of some different spheres such as basketballs, baseballs, beach balls, golf balls, and so on. What is the ratio of circumference to diameter for spheres? Is it the same as it was for circles?
- How could you find the circumference and diameter of Earth? Of the moon?

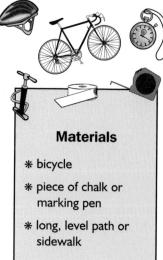

Experiment 11

Another Way to Measure Distance with Your Bike

In Experiment 9 you found that you could measure distance by counting the number of rotations of your bicycle wheel. To avoid danger, you were advised not to ride your bike while you counted. There is another way to measure distance with your bicycle. It is better for measuring long distances because you can ride as you count. This method involves finding out how far your bicycle travels with each turn of the pedals, just as you did in Experiment 7, rather than with each turn of the wheels. For a more accurate measurement, use your hand to move the bike forward by turning the pedal around five times. Then measure the distance your bike has traveled. How far does the bike move with each pedal turn? How can you measure distance by counting pedal turns? If you have a bicycle with multiple gears, how does the gear the bike is in affect the distance it travels for each turn of the pedals?

Under what conditions will this method not work?

As you learned in Chapter 2, a bicycle's gear, in gear-inches, is *related* to the distance its wheels travel with each turn of the pedals, but it is not *equal* to that distance. A bicycle's gear-inches is given by the equation

$$\text{gear-inches} = \frac{\text{number of teeth on front sprocket gear}}{\text{number of teeth on rear sprocket gear}} \times \text{wheel diameter (in inches)}$$

Based on what you found in Experiment 10, you can find the distance a bicycle travels with each turn of the pedals by multiplying the gear-inches by pi (π), or about 3.14. Explain why the distance the bike travels per pedal turn in a particular gear is equal to π times the gear-inches.

How can you find the distance a bike will travel for any number of turns of the pedals?

Science Project Idea

How can you use number of pedal turns, gear-inches, π, and time to find a bicycle's speed?

Experiment 12

Measuring Your Bicycle's Speed

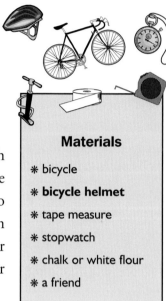

Materials

* bicycle
* **bicycle helmet**
* tape measure
* stopwatch
* chalk or white flour
* a friend

You can measure the speed at which you pedal your bike by using a tape measure and a stopwatch. To do this, make two marks about 50 m (165 feet) apart on a level path or sidewalk. Chalk or some white flour can be used to make the marks.

Be sure you are wearing your bicycle helmet. Ride at a steady speed on your bicycle before you reach the first of the two marks. When you reach the first mark, yell, *Go!* Have a friend with a stopwatch stand at the second position you have marked. When your friend hears you yell *Go,* she will start the stopwatch. Your friend will stop the watch at the moment your bike's handlebars pass the second mark.

From the elapsed time on the stopwatch and the distance between the two marks, you can calculate your speed. Your speed was the distance you traveled divided by the time to travel that distance.

$$\text{speed} = \frac{\text{distance}}{\text{time}}$$

Suppose it took you 12.5 seconds to travel the 50 meters between the two marks. Your speed would be

$$\text{speed} = \frac{50 \text{ m}}{12.5 \text{ s}} = 4.0 \text{ m/s}$$

If you wanted to express your speed in kilometers per hour (km/h), you know from Table 1 that there are 1,000 meters in a kilometer and 3,600 seconds in an hour. Therefore, 1 m/s is equal to 1/1,000 km ÷ 1/3,600 h (0.001 km/0.0002778 h), or 3.6 km/h. Consequently, your speed in kilometers per hour would be

$$4.0 \text{ m/s} \times \frac{3.6 \text{ km/h}}{1 \text{ m/s}} = 14.4 \text{ km/h}$$

What would be the speed in miles per hour? (Remember, a mile is equal to 1.61 kilometers.) If you measured the speed in feet per second, how could you change it to miles per hour?

Science Project Ideas

- If your bicycle has a speedometer, does the speedometer on your bicycle agree with the speedometer on your family's car? **With an adult to help you**, how can you find out?
- Find out how the speedometer on your bicycle works. How accurately does it measure speed? How does the odometer (the part that measures distance) work? How accurately does it measure distance?
- How can you use a stopwatch and a speedometer to test the accuracy of a bike's odometer?

Experiment 13

Measuring Your Bicycle's Speed with Water Balloons

Materials

* chalk or white flour

* level walk, path, or sidewalk

* water

* balloons

* bicycle (speedometer optional)

* **bicycle helmet**

* meterstick, yardstick, or tape measure

* a friend

* stopwatch

You can also measure your speed on a bicycle in a less direct but more interesting way. Use some chalk or a little white flour to make a target near one side of a level walk, path, or sidewalk. Next, fill some balloons with water. Seal them by tying off the necks.

Be sure that no one is walking along the path or sidewalk. When the path is clear and while **wearing your bicycle helmet,** hold the balloon against one handlebar of your bike as you ride by the target (see Figure 14). Plan your approach so that the balloon will be directly over the bull's-eye as you ride over the target. Release the water balloon at the moment it is directly above the target.

Return to the scene of your experiment. Did the water balloon land on the target? If not, where did it strike the ground? Can you explain why it landed where it did and not on the target?

Try the experiment several times at different speeds. Each time, release the water-filled balloon when it is directly over

Figure 14. Release a water "bomb" from a moving bicycle when the bomb is directly over a target. Where will the bomb strike the ground?

the target. How does your bike's speed affect the horizontal distance the balloon travels before it hits the ground?

Repeat the experiment, but this time ask a friend to ride the bike and drop the water balloon. Meanwhile, you should stand next to the target a short distance from the path. Watch the water balloon as it falls. Does it continue to move with the bike as it falls, or does it fall straight down from the point at which it is released?

By measuring the distance a water balloon travels after you release it from your bicycle, you can actually measure how fast your bike was going at the time you released the water balloon. The reason you can is that the time for any heavy object, such as a water balloon, to fall a given distance is always the same. The time, in seconds, for a heavy object to fall through a known height measured in meters is always very nearly equal to the square root of two-tenths (0.2) the height; that is:

$$\text{time in seconds} = \sqrt{0.2 \times \text{height in meters}}$$

If the height is measured in feet, the time, in seconds, is very nearly equal to the square root of 1/16th (0.0625) the height; that is:

$$\text{time in seconds} = \sqrt{0.0625 \times \text{height in feet}}$$

Using a calculator with a square root key, you can calculate the time very easily. For example, if you drop the water balloon from a height of 90 cm (0.90 m), the time for it to reach the ground will be

$$\text{time} = \sqrt{0.2 \times 0.90} = \sqrt{0.18 \text{ s}^2} = 0.42 \text{ s}$$

If that same height is measured in feet, the time is given by

$$\text{time} = \sqrt{.0625 \times 2.95} = 0.43 \text{ s}$$

(The difference in time [0.01 second] between the two calculations is the result of rounding off 0.204 to 0.2 when the distance was measured in meters.)

As you have found, the water balloon continues to move horizontally along with the bicycle after you release it. That is why it always lands some distance beyond the target.

It was Galileo who first realized that a moving object dropped from a height maintains its horizontal speed after it is released. He did an experiment somewhat similar to yours. He had a sailor climb to the top of the mast of a moving ship and release a small weight. The weight did not fall behind the ship. It landed at the base of the mast from which it was dropped, showing that it continued to move with the ship's horizontal speed as it fell.

When Sir Isaac Newton formulated his three laws of motion, Galileo's discovery became part of his first law. This law states that a moving object maintains its speed in the direction it is moving unless a force acts on it.

In Galileo's experiment, there was no force that could change the object's horizontal velocity once the sailor released it. The force of gravity pulled the object downward, but it did not change its horizontal speed. Galileo used his experiment to show that changes in horizontal and vertical velocities are independent of one another. As he demonstrated later, the vertical (downward) velocity of a falling object increases as it falls. Its horizontal velocity, however, remains unchanged unless something pushes it forward or backward as it falls.

Using Newton's first law of motion, you can determine the speed of your bike at the moment you release a water balloon. Have a friend stand near the target as you do the experiment. Your friend can do two things: (1) watch carefully to be certain that you release the water balloon at a point directly over the target, and (2) mark the exact point where the water balloon lands. Because water-filled balloons splash when they land, your friend may have difficulty marking the exact point where the balloon strikes the ground. If that is the case, try dropping a small, sealed, cotton bag that contains a stone and some white flour.

Once you have done the experiment, you and your friend can measure the distance between the target, which is where you released the water balloon, and the point where it lands. Divide that distance by the time to fall through the height from which it was released to find the bike's velocity, which was also the horizontal velocity of the water balloon. You can find the speed in either meters per second (m/s) or feet per second (ft/s).

Suppose you released the water balloon from a height of 80 cm (0.8 m), and it landed 1.2 m beyond the point from which it was dropped.

The time to fall 0.8 m is

$$t = \sqrt{0.2 \times 0.8} = \sqrt{0.16} = 0.40 \text{ s}$$

The speed of the bike, then, would be

$$v = \frac{1.2 \text{ m}}{0.40 \text{ s}} = 3.0 \text{ m/s}$$

If your bike has a speedometer, you can compare your calculation of speed with that of the bike's speedometer. The speedometer probably measures speed in kilometers per hour (km/h) or miles per hour (mph), so you will have to convert km/h to m/s or mph to ft/s. A calculator will make these calculations easy.

To change km/h to m/s, you need to know that a kilometer is 1,000 meters and an hour is 3,600 seconds. So, 1 km/h = 0.28 m/s, because

$$1 \text{ km/h} = 1,000 \text{ m}/3,600 \text{ s} = 0.28 \text{ m/s}$$

Thus, a speed of 20 km/h, for example, is the same speed as 5.6 m/s, because

$$20 \text{ km/h} \times 0.28 \text{ m/s for each km/s} = 5.6 \text{ m/s}$$

To change mph to ft/s you need to know that a mile is 5,280 feet and an hour is 3,600 seconds. Therefore, a speed of 1 mph = 1.47 ft/s, because

1 mph = 5,280 ft/3,600 s = 1.47 ft/s

Thus, a speed of 12 mph is the same speed as 17.6 ft/s, because

12 mph × 1.47 ft/s for each mph = 17.6 ft/s

How closely does your speed as measured by your speedometer agree with your speed as measured by the falling water balloon?

Chapter 4

Forces Every Cyclist Must Overcome or Apply

The first part of Newton's first law of motion tells us that a body in motion maintains its speed and direction of motion. It would be an easy ride indeed if all you had to do was get started on your bike and let Newton's first law take over. You would just continue to roll along at the same speed and in the same direction without ever having to pedal.

There is, however, a second part to Newton's first law. The entire law states that a body in motion maintains its speed and direction of motion *unless acted upon by an unbalanced force.* Those forces that act on you, me, and everything else are always with us. We try to pedal up a steep hill and the force of gravity causes our speed to decrease.

If we are going down the hill, gravity pulls on us and our speed increases, even when we do not pedal.

Newton's second law describes what happens when an unbalanced force does act. It tells us that when such a force acts on an object, that object accelerates; that is, its velocity changes. The speed may increase or decrease, or the object may change direction, depending on which way the force pushes or pulls the object. When you are going uphill, for example, the force of gravity acts to reduce your speed; the same force acts to increase your speed if you are going downhill. Furthermore, this second law tells us that the acceleration is proportional to the total force that acts on the object and inversely proportional to the mass of the object. This means that if the force doubles, the acceleration doubles. If the amount of matter (which is what mass is) in the object doubles, the acceleration is halved.

In an ideal world, if you gave an object a small push, it would accelerate while you pushed on it. Once you stopped pushing, it would continue to move in the same direction at a constant speed until another force acted on it. In the real world, there is a type of force that almost always opposes motion. That force is friction.

Even though friction opposes motion, we cannot move without it. If you tried to walk or ride your bike on a frictionless surface, you could not move. You may have experienced something very close to a frictionless surface if you have tried to walk on very smooth, slightly wet ice. It is only because we are able to push back against the ground with our feet or with a bicycle's tire that we can move forward. The fact that we move forward only when we push back is explained by Newton's third law of motion. The third law states, "To every action there is an equal and opposite reaction." This means, for example, that when you push back against the earth with your foot, the earth exerts an equal force forward on your foot.

In the next experiment, you will find the force of friction that opposes the motion of your bicycle.

Experiment 14

Friction and Your Bicycle

Spring scales, like the one you may have used in Experiment 3 (see Figure 15a), can be used to measure forces. Since friction is a force, we should be able to measure it with a spring scale.

To find the frictional force that opposes the motion of your bicycle, begin by tying a heavy string around the front part of your bike's frame. Attach the string to a spring scale. You will use the scale to pull the bike forward at a slow but steady speed along a smooth, level surface. As long as the speed is constant, the force you exert will be just enough to overcome friction. Have a friend keep your bicycle upright without pushing it or pressing down on it, while you pull the bike forward, as shown in Figure 15b. According to the spring scale, what is the frictional force that opposes the motion of your riderless bicycle? What happens to the bike's speed when you pull with a force greater than the force of friction?

Friction on Different Surfaces

Repeat the experiment with the bike on different level surfaces. You might try it on macadam (blacktop pavement), concrete, dirt, gravel, grass, sand, and other surfaces. Is the

Materials

* spring scale
* bicycle
* heavy string
* a friend
* different smooth, level surfaces such as macadam, concrete, dirt, gravel, grass, and sand
* a heavy person
* a light person
* tire gauge
* bicycle tire pump

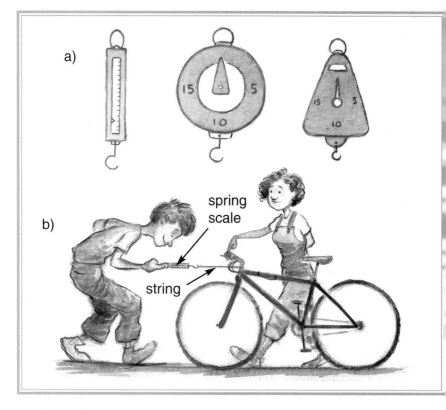

Figure 15. a) Any of these spring scales can be used to measure forces. b) How much friction is there between your bike's tires and the surface over which it rolls?

frictional force that acts on your bicycle related to the surface over which the bike rolls? If it is, on which surface is the friction greatest? On which surface is friction the least?

Friction and Weight

How does weight affect the frictional force on your bicycle? To find out, have your friend sit on the bike as you pull it with a spring scale along a smooth, level surface at a small but constant speed. Is the force the same, greater, or less than it was when you pulled the bike without anyone on it?

Suppose someone much heavier than your friend sits on the bike while you pull it with a spring scale. Do you think the friction between the bike and the surface over which it rolls will be the same, greater, or less than it was when your lighter friend was on the bike? Try it. Were you right? Why must you do this experiment on the same surface you used when you pulled your first friend along?

Suppose someone who weighs much less than your first friend sits on the bike while you pull it with the spring scale. Do you think the friction between the bike and the surface over which it rolls will be the same, greater, or less than it was when your friend was on the bike? Try it. Were you right?

Suppose you pull your bike, with your first friend on board, along different surfaces such as those you tried before (macadam, concrete, dirt, gravel, grass, sand, etc.). Do you think the frictional force will be different on different surfaces? If you do, try to predict what those forces will be. Were your predictions close to the actual force measurements you made?

Friction and Tire Pressure

Does the pressure of the tires affect the force of friction? To find out, ask a friend to sit on your bicycle. Then use a spring scale to pull him or her along a smooth, level surface at a small but steady speed. With what force do you have to pull the bike and your friend to overcome friction? Next, use a tire gauge to measure the air pressure in the tires. Reduce that pressure to about 4/5 of what it was and repeat the experiment. Do you find any change in the frictional force acting on the bicycle?

Repeat the experiment at about 3/5, then 2/5, and finally 1/5 of its original pressure. Using axes like those shown in Figure 16, plot a graph of the frictional force on your bicycle versus the air pressure in the tires. What do you conclude?

Finally, use a bicycle pump to reinflate your tires to the proper pressure.

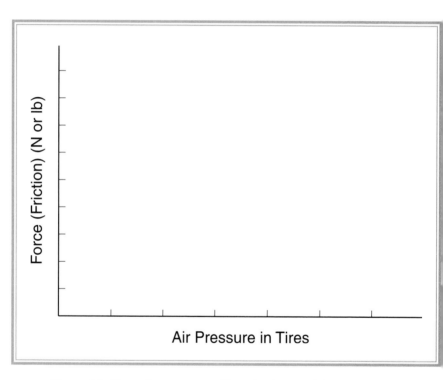

Figure 16. Does tire pressure affect the frictional force acting on your bicycle?

Science Project Ideas

- Does the width of the tires affect the frictional force acting on the bicycle? Design and carry out an experiment to find out.
- Does the diameter of the tires affect the frictional force acting on the bicycle? Design and carry out an experiment to find out.
- In Experiment 14 you measured rolling friction. The wheel was free to turn as you pulled the bike along a level surface. Design and carry out an experiment to measure sliding friction; that is, to find the force needed to slide the bicycle forward at a steady speed when the wheels cannot turn. How does sliding friction compare with rolling friction?

Experiment 15

Bicycle Wheels and Ball Bearings

Materials

* bicycle
* old bike that has been discarded (optional)

In Experiment 5 you saw how ball bearings reduce friction. In this experiment you will see how important they are in your bicycle.

Turn your bicycle upside down so that it rests on the handlebars and seat. Then give the front wheel a pull to make it spin. Notice how easily it turns and for sooo-ooo long!

The reason your bicycle wheel spins so easily is because its axle turns on ball bearings. For the same reason, your bike pedals turn very easily, especially if you remove the chain from the front sprocket. The axle connecting the cranks that attach to the pedals turn on ball bearings.

If you can find an old bike that has been discarded, you might like to take the wheels and/or the cranks and front sprocket apart so that you can see the ball bearings that reduce friction to a minimum. Another approach might be to visit a bicycle repair shop. You could ask the owner for permission to watch while a repair is done on a part that exposes the ball bearings.

How many ball bearings do you see? How large are they? On what do the bearings turn?

Experiment 16

Pedal Positions and the Driving Force on a Bicycle

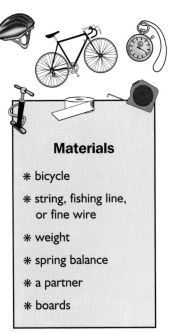

Materials

* bicycle
* string, fishing line, or fine wire
* weight
* spring balance
* a partner
* boards

Normally, the force that makes your bicycle move comes from you pushing on the pedals. But as you know, pushing down on a pedal at some positions has little or no effect on the bicycle. So how is the force that drives a bicycle forward related to the position of the pedal when you push on it?

To find out, you can use string, fishing line, or fine wire to hang a known weight on a pedal as shown in Figure 17a. Attach a spring scale to the bicycle frame. Hold the scale in a horizontal position (see Figure 17b). It will enable you to measure the forward force on the bicycle when the weighted pedal is at different angles. A partner can keep the bicycle upright, being careful not to exert any force that would move the bike forward or backward. If the weight hangs so far below the pedal that it strikes the ground at certain angles, you can place the front and rear wheels on stacks of boards. In that way, the weight can hang well below the pedal without touching the ground even at its lowest point.

At what position does the pedal produce the largest forward force on the bicycle? At what position or positions does the pedal exert no forward force on the bicycle?

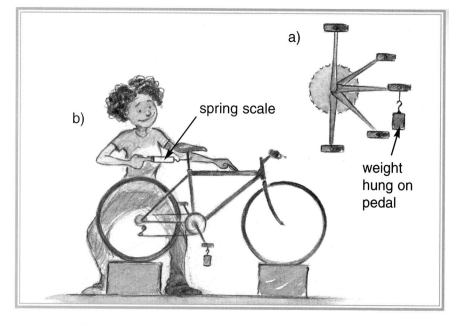

Figure 17. a) Hang a weight from the pedal. The pedal can then be set at different angles. b) Use a spring scale to measure the forward force on the bicycle when the weighted pedal is at various positions. Both wheels can be elevated to prevent the weight from touching the ground.

From Coaster Brakes to Machines, Forces, and Work

You may remember from Chapter 1 that coaster brakes, found on most bicycles in the middle of the twentieth century, were inefficient. To see why that is true, you need to first examine what is meant by mechanical advantage, work, and efficiency.

A bicycle is a complex machine that is made of many simple machines. There are six basic types of machines: the inclined plane, the wedge, the lever, the wheel and axle, the pulley, and the screw. Examples of these simple machines are shown in Figure 18.

Humans invented machines to make their work easier or to change the direction of a force used to do work. For

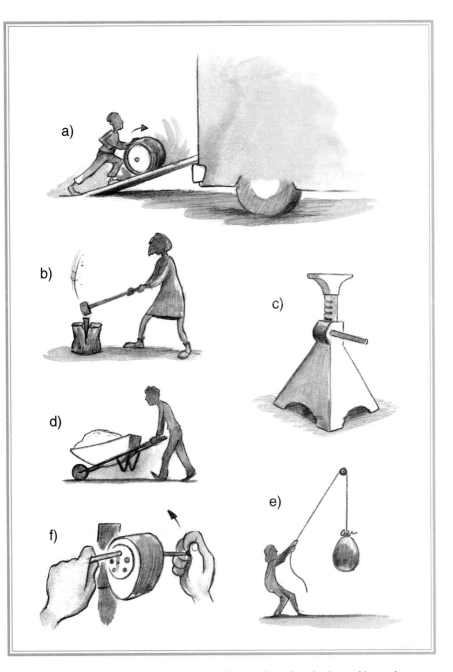

Figure 18. Examples of simple machines: a) inclined plane; b) wedge; c) screw; d) levers; e) pulley; f) wheel and axle. How many simple machines can you find on your bicycle?

example, the pulley in Figure 18e allows the worker to lift the weight by pulling down rather than risking a back injury by bending over to lift it. A lever, such as the wheelbarrow shown in Figure 18d, allows a person to apply a larger or smaller force to an object than the one he or she could exert at another point on the lever.

You may wonder how a machine can magnify a force. Doesn't that break some kind of scientific law, such as conservation of energy? The answer is no! The reason is that the work the person does (the energy he or she provides) is always more than the work output of the machine. To see why, look at the boy pushing down on the lever in Figure 19. He exerts a force of 100 newtons (22.5 pounds) at a distance of 1.0 m from the fulcrum in order to lift a weight of 400 newtons (90 pounds) that is 0.25 m from the fulcrum. The boy's mechanical advantage is 4.0 because the output force (the force that lifts the weight) of 400 N is 4 times greater than the input force of 100 N that the boy exerts. By definition,

$$\text{mechanical advantage} = \frac{\text{output force}}{\text{input force}}$$

But the work done on something is defined as the force acting on the object times the distance through which the force acts. The boy has to push downward through a distance of 0.4 m in order to raise the weight 0.1 m. Consequently, the work done by the boy (the work input) is

$$100 \text{ N} \times 0.4 \text{ m} = 40 \text{ N-m or 40 joules}$$

(One joule [J] is equal to one newton-meter.)

The work done on the weight (the work output) is

$$400 \text{ N} \times 0.1 \text{ m} = 40 \text{ N-m or 40 J}$$

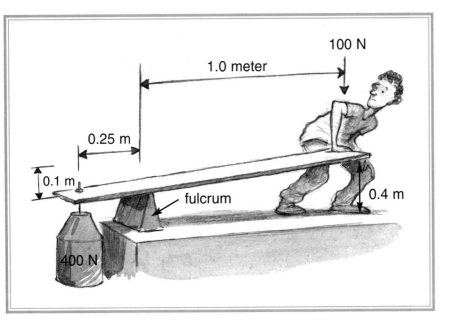

Figure 19. To lift a 400-N weight 0.1 m, the boy exerts a force of 100 N through a distance of 0.4 m. The work done on the weight is 400 N × 0.1 m = 40 J. How much work does the boy do?

Actually, the work done by the boy will be more than the work done on the weight because the boy has to overcome frictional forces between the lever and the fulcrum that oppose the force he exerts. For example, the force he exerts might actually be 104 N. If that were the case, the work input would exceed the work output by 1.6 J because

104 N × 0.4 m = 41.6 J, and 41.6 J – 40 J = 1.6 J

Efficiency is defined as the ratio of work output to work input. In this case, the efficiency would be

$$\frac{\text{work output}}{\text{work input}} = \frac{40\text{ J}}{41.6\text{ J}} = 0.96 \text{ or } 96\ \%$$

So what has all this to do with coaster brakes and efficiency? The next experiment should help you answer that question.

Experiment 17

Bikes, Brakes, and Levers

Materials

* ✷ bicycle with a coaster brake
* ✷ bicycle with hand brakes
* ✷ 2 spring scales
* ✷ heavy object such as doorstop, wedge, or brick
* ✷ tape
* ✷ string
* ✷ ruler
* ✷ a partner
* ✷ a long pin
* ✷ plastic drinking straw
* ✷ 2 identical small metal cans or drinking mugs
* ✷ fine felt-tip pen
* ✷ paper clips
* ✷ notebook

Bikes that have balloon tires and a single gear on both front and rear sprockets usually have a coaster brake. You may notice that the rear hub on these bikes is larger than the hub on most bicycles. The reason is that there is a brake mechanism inside the hub that retards the rotation of the axle. To make the coaster brake work, a rider pushes backward on the pedals. The chain, in turn, pushes back on the rear sprocket, which causes the brake inside the hub to push against the axle and reduce the bike's speed.

You can compare a coaster brake with the hand-operated brakes on most multi-geared bicycles. In hand-operated brakes, a system of levers connected by strong wires squeezes hard rubber brake pads against the rims of the bike's wheels. There is a brake for both the rear wheel and the front wheel.

There are several ways to compare these two braking systems. One way is to try to turn the rear wheel of a bike with a coaster brake while the brake is on. Then try to turn the wheel of a multi-speed bike while the hand brake squeezes the brake pads firmly against the wheel's rim. In which case is the wheel easier to turn? Can you explain why?

The major difference between these two braking systems is the place where the force is applied to the wheel. The coaster brake acts on the axle of the wheel. With the multi-speed bike, the braking force acts on the rim of the wheel. You can feel the difference between these two braking mechanisms. First, grasp the spokes of a bicycle wheel close to the hub with your right hand. Grasp the tire of the same wheel with your left hand. Now try to prevent the wheel from turning with your right hand while you turn the wheel slowly with your left hand. Can you prevent the wheel from turning? (Be careful not to bend the spokes.)

Repeat the experiment, but this time grasp the *rim* of the wheel with your right hand. You will find it much easier to stop the turning action of your left hand. About how much harder do you have to pull to turn the wheel when your braking hand (right hand) is on the rim instead of on the axle?

For a more quantitative experiment, use a spring scale to find the weight of a heavy object such as a wedge, a doorstop, or a brick. Tape the heavy object to the tire of an inverted bicycle as shown in Figure 20. Tape a string to the tire on the opposite side of the wheel. Using a spring scale, measure the force on the spring needed to balance the wheel and keep it from turning. How does the force compare with the weight of the object?

Next, measure the force needed to keep the wheel from turning when the scale is connected to a spoke near the hub of the wheel (see Figure 20). Finally, measure the force needed

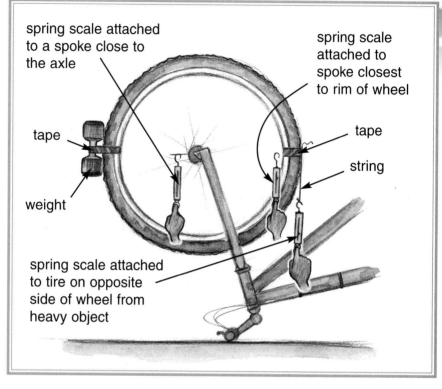

spring scale attached to a spoke close to the axle

spring scale attached to spoke closest to rim of wheel

tape

tape

string

weight

spring scale attached to tire on opposite side of wheel from heavy object

Figure 20. A coaster brake acts on a wheel's axle. Why is it better to have a brake that acts on the rim of the wheel?

to keep the wheel from turning when the scale is attached to a spoke near the rim of the wheel.

As you have found, forces applied at different points along the radius of a wheel behave much like those acting on a lever. To see this more directly, attach strings to spokes on opposite sides of the wheel. Place one string 20 cm from the center of the wheel. Place the other string 10 cm from the center on the opposite side of the wheel, as shown in Figure 21. Attach spring scales to the strings. Pull on one spring while a friend pulls on the other so that the wheel does not turn. You will find that the force 20 cm from the center is just half as large as the balancing force 10 cm from the center. What mechanical advantage does this setup provide?

To see the corresponding arrangement on a lever, push a pin across the exact center of a drinking straw at a point above the midline, as shown in Figure 22a. Place the ends of the pin on the edges of two identical small metal cans or drinking mugs, as shown in Figure 22b. The pin should balance in a level (or nearly level) position on the cans.

Use a fine felt-tip pen to make marks at 1.0-cm intervals outward along the straw from its center. Make marks on both

Figure 21. A bicycle wheel, which is a simple wheel and axle, can serve as a machine.

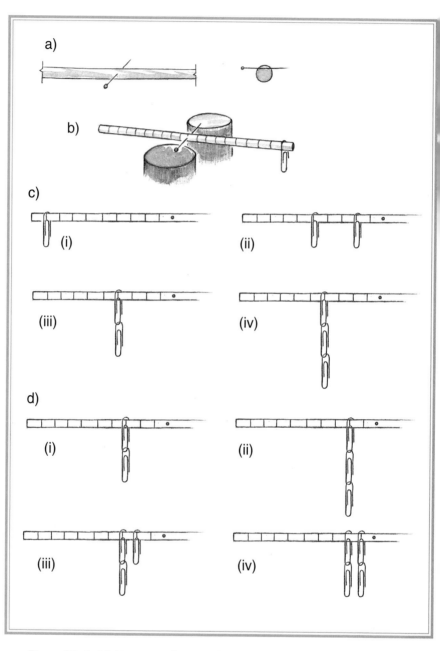

Figure 22. A drinking-straw lever with its fulcrum at its center can be used to search for a law of levers. Does the same law apply to a bicycle wheel?

sides of the straw, as shown in Figure 22b. Hang a paper clip at the mark closest to one end of the straw. (If the paper clip slides along the straw, pinch it so that it grips the straw slightly.) Where can you hang a second paper clip to balance the straw? Where can you hang two paper clips to make the straw balance?

Figure 22c shows some drawings of one side of a straw that is level (balanced). There are two paper clips on the other side of the straw. Use two paper clips to find out how the other side of the straw looks. Then make drawings that show both sides of all the straws shown in Figure 22c.

Figure 22d shows one side of four different straws that are balanced. Only one paper clip is on the other side of the straw. Draw a picture showing both sides of each balanced straw.

Continue to experiment with the straw and paper clips until you can develop a mathematical rule that will allow you to predict any balanced position for an equal-arm lever.

Experiment 18

A Bicycle-Wheel Centrifuge

A centrifuge is a device used by chemists to make insoluble particles settle out of solution faster. A test tube containing a mixture of solid and liquid is placed in the centrifuge. The centrifuge then spins around at high speed. The bottom of the test tube is farthest from the center of the machine so that the heavier solid particles, which are "thrown" outward by the spinning motion, wind up at the bottom of the tube.

Materials

* fine starch or flour
* clear **plastic** vial or pill bottle with a cap (**do not use glass**)
* water
* bicycle
* heavy blocks to support bicycle on its side
* tape
* muddy water
* cooking oil in soapy water

You can prepare a mixture of a liquid and an insoluble solid by adding some fine starch or flour to a clear plastic vial or pill bottle that is three quarters filled with water. Put a cap on the container and shake it. Notice how slowly the particles settle to the bottom of the vial.

To increase the rate at which the solid separates from the liquid, you can turn your bicycle wheel into a centrifuge. Put the bike in its highest gear, turn it on its side, and support it on some heavy blocks. Then tape the capped vial to spokes near the rim of the wheel, as shown in Figure 23. Use a pedal to spin the wheel at high speed for about 10 seconds. Then

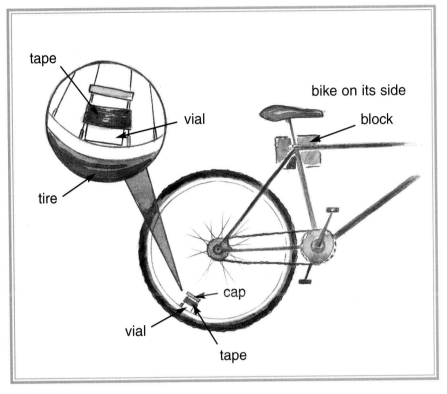

Figure 23. A bicycle wheel can be used as a centrifuge.

stop the wheel and look at the vial. What has happened to the starch or flour particles?

Can you use your bicycle centrifuge to turn muddy water clear? Can you use it to separate cooking oil mixed with soapy water?

Chapter 5

Working on Your Bicycle

Your bicycle, as you know, is a machine made up of many smaller simple machines. A bicycle wheel, as you will see, could be used as a wheel and axle. In this chapter you will also learn how you can use the concept of work to measure the force opposing the motion of your bicycle, and how gravity can be used to do work on you and your bike. You will also discover whether or not you are as powerful as a horse.

Experiment 19
Bikes, Mechanical Advantage, Work, and Efficiency

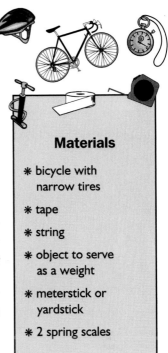

Materials

* ✳ bicycle with narrow tires
* ✳ tape
* ✳ string
* ✳ object to serve as a weight
* ✳ meterstick or yardstick
* ✳ 2 spring scales

Turn a bicycle with narrow tires upside down. Tape one end of a short string to the front tire. Tie one end of a longer string to the end of a spoke next to the front axle. Then wrap the string once or twice around the axle next to the spoke. Attach an object of known weight to the free end of the string, as shown in Figure 24.

Next, use a meterstick or yardstick to measure the diameter of the axle and the radius of the wheel. Based on the radii of the wheel and axle, what is the theoretical mechanical advantage of this machine (the bicycle wheel) if the weight attached to the axle is raised by applying a force to the wheel? You can think of the wheel and axle as a circular lever.

Use a spring scale to measure the force that must be applied to the tire to balance the weight attached to the axle. What is the actual mechanical advantage of this machine? How much work, in joules, would have to be done to raise the weight from the ground to the axle? Remember, work is force times the distance through which the force acts.

Remove the weight and wrap the string around the axle a few times so that when you reconnect the weight it will be several centimeters off the ground. Measure the exact distance between the bottom of the weight and the ground. Predict the

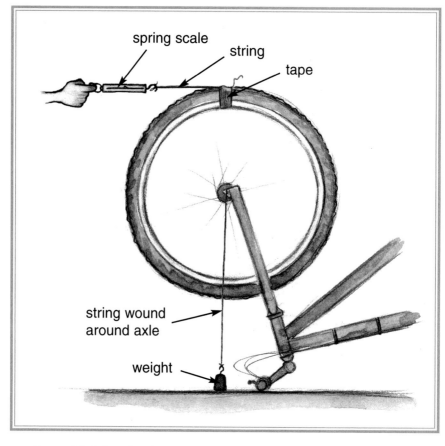

Figure 24. A bicycle wheel can serve as a wheel-and-axle machine. What mechanical advantage can it provide? How efficient is it?

distance between the weight and the ground if you wrap the string around the axle ten more times. Remember, the circumference of the axle is its diameter times pi (π).

How many times would you have to rotate the wheel to lift the weight from the ground to the axle? What is the wheel's diameter? What is its circumference? Through what distance does the force you apply to the wheel move each time you turn the wheel around once? How much *actual* work would you have to do to lift the weight from the ground to the axle using the wheel? If the weight were simply lifted straight up from ground to axle, how much work would have to be done? What is the efficiency of the bicycle wheel as a wheel-and-axle machine?

You can use the same upside-down bicycle to do an additional experiment. Start with the bike in its lowest gear. Use string and tape to attach one spring scale to a pedal and a second to the rear tire. Pull on the pedal with a force that extends the spring scale to a point near its maximum reading. Have a friend pull on the wheel with a second spring scale. What force on the wheel is needed to keep it from turning? How do you know that the force that keeps the wheel from turning is equal to, but opposite in direction from, the force that wants to turn the wheel? What is the ratio of the force on the pedal to the force on the wheel?

If the pedal were to make one complete turn, how much work would be done on the pedal, assuming the force on the pedal was constant? How much work would be done on the wheel? What is the efficiency of the bike under these conditions? Why will the actual efficiency be less?

Repeat the experiment with the bicycle in a medium gear and in its highest gear. What is the mechanical advantage in each case? How much work would be done for each turn of the pedals, assuming the force on the pedals was constant? How much work would be done on the wheel? What is the efficiency of the bike under each of these conditions? Assume you are going to use the pedal and wheel to lift a weight attached to the rear wheel's tire. Which rear gear would you use to lift a really heavy weight?

Bikes, Work, and Kinetic Energy

When work is done on an object, that object acquires energy. You do work even when you pedal your bicycle along a level path. The sweat on your brow tells you that! Because of the work you do, you and your bike acquire energy. The energy you acquire is the energy of motion, which is called kinetic energy. The kinetic energy of a stationary object is zero because it has no motion. The kinetic energy, in joules, of a moving object is equal to 1/2 its mass, *m*, (in kg) times its velocity, *v*, (in m/s) squared. In terms of a formula, kinetic energy is equal to $1/2 \, mv^2$. That is,

$$KE = 1/2 \, mv^2$$

To take away an object's kinetic energy, you must do an equivalent amount of work on it, so that

$$\text{work} = \text{force} \times \text{distance} = 1/2 \, mv^2$$

You know how to measure velocity. An object's mass, which is the amount of matter in it, is easy to measure—just put the object on a balance. Most scientists measure mass in kilograms and force in newtons. In U.S. customary units, force is measured in pounds and mass is measured in slugs. You have heard of pounds, but you may have never heard of slugs, at least not as a unit to measure mass.

Experiment 20

Another Way to Measure the Frictional Force on a Bike

Materials

* bathroom scale
* a long, level surface
* bicycle
* **bicycle helmet**
* stick or other means of making a mark to represent a starting line
* speedometer on bike or a tape measure, a friend, and a stopwatch

You can use the concept of work and kinetic energy to measure the frictional force acting on your bicycle. Suppose you know the velocity with which your bike is moving as you ride on a long, level path. If you know your mass and the mass of the bike, you can find the kinetic energy of the bike with you on it. For example, if you and your bike together weigh 50 kg and you are riding along at 10 m/s, your (you and your bike's) kinetic energy is

$$1/2 \; mv^2 = 1/2 \; (50 \text{ kg}) \times (10 \text{ m/s})^2 = 2{,}500 \text{ joules}$$

To carry out the experiment, ride at a steady speed. Then, beginning at some marked point, let the bike coast until it comes to rest. The work done in slowing and stopping you and the bike is equal to the force acting against the bike's motion times the distance through which that force acts.

Try to do this experiment when there is little or no wind. A crosswind will not have much effect on your results, but a head- or tailwind will provide an unwanted force.

To find the total mass of you and your bicycle, hold your bicycle off the ground or floor while you stand on a bathroom scale. If the scale readings are in pounds, you can find the mass in kilograms by dividing the number of pounds by 2.2. For example, if the scale reads 150 pounds, the mass of you and your bicycle is

$$\frac{150 \text{ lb}}{2.2} = 68 \text{ kg}$$

Find a long, level surface and make a mark at some point along the path to serve as a starting point. You will need to know your speed as you cross the starting line. If your bike has a speedometer, all you need to do is note the speed as you cross the starting point. If you do not have a speedometer, you can measure the speed as you did in Experiment 12, with a friend using a stopwatch and a tape measure. In either case, you should begin coasting at a slow speed—15 km/h (9 mph) or less—so that air resistance can be ignored.

After coasting to a stop, you will need to measure the distance you traveled. From the distance the bike rolled, the mass of you and your bike, and the speed when you started coasting, you can calculate the force acting against the bike's motion, because

$$\text{work} = \text{force} \times \text{distance} = 1/2 \ mv^2$$

Consequently, since equals divided by equals are one,

$$\frac{\text{force} \times \cancel{\text{distance}}}{\cancel{\text{distance}}} = \frac{1/2 \ mv^2}{\text{distance}}, \text{ or force} = \frac{1/2 \ mv^2}{\text{distance}}$$

For example, let's suppose the mass of you and your bicycle was 68 kg, your speed as you crossed the starting line was 10 mph, and you coasted 100 m. Since a mile is 1.6 km, your speed, in km/h, was 16 km/h. There are 3,600 seconds in an hour, so your speed, in m/s, was

$$16,000 \text{ m}/3,600 \text{ s} = 4.4 \text{ m/s}$$

Your kinetic energy was

$$1/2 \, mv^2 = 1/2 \times 68 \text{ kg} \times (4.4 \text{ m/s})^2 = 660 \text{ N-m or } 660 \text{ J}$$

You coasted 100 m, so the average force acting against your motion must have been

$$\text{force} = \frac{1/2 \, mv^2}{\text{distance}} = \frac{660 \text{ N-m}}{100 \text{ m}} = 6.6 \text{ N}$$

Using your data, what do you find was the frictional force acting on your bike? How does this compare with the value you found for the friction acting against the bicycle in Experiment 14? Why might the two values be different? What assumption have we made about the force acting on the bicycle?

To investigate the effect of air resistance on you and your bike, repeat the experiment at higher speeds. At higher speeds you can feel the air pushing against you with more force. How does air resistance change your results? How can you tell what part of the force is due to air resistance and what part is due to friction on the tires?

Science Project Ideas

- Design and carry out an experiment to measure the frictional force between the ball bearings and the axle that turns on them in a bicycle wheel.
  - Design and carry out an experiment that will allow you to compensate for any wind you might encounter in doing Experiment 20.

Gravitational Potential Energy, You, and Your Bike

An object in a position above the ground has gravitational potential energy. It has potential energy because it has the potential to do work. It is gravitational potential energy because it is the force of gravity that enables it to do work. The force of gravity acts on the object and, if the object falls freely through a height, it can do work. The amount of work it can do is equal to the force of gravity (the weight of the object) times the distance through which that force acts. The height something falls is, of course, the distance through which the force of gravity acts on it. Consequently, the work the object can do is equal to its weight times the height through which it falls. That is,

potential energy = weight × height = work that can be done

In the next experiment, you will use your own gravitational potential energy to do work on your bike and yourself. You will let your weight push the bike's pedal downward through some height. Some of the work you do will appear as kinetic energy. By measuring the work you do and the kinetic energy that results, you can determine how efficiently you transfer energy. Remember:

$$\text{efficiency} = \frac{\text{energy (or work) output}}{\text{energy (or work) input}}$$

Experiment 21

Work, Kinetic Energy, Efficiency, and Your Bike

Materials

* bicycle
* **bicycle helmet**
* ruler
* a friend
* speedometer or a tape measure and a stopwatch
* bathroom scale

When you pedal your bike, you do work on both it and yourself. Both you and your bike acquire kinetic energy. To find out how efficiently you transfer energy, first determine how far your bicycle pedal falls vertically when it goes from its highest to its lowest position. One way to do this is to measure the distance from the ground to the bottom of the pedal when it is in its highest and lowest positions. The difference between these two heights is the vertical distance the pedal moves.

If you apply your full weight to the pedal as it moves from its highest to its lowest position, you do work on the bike. And you do work on yourself because both you and your bicycle gain kinetic energy. This kinetic energy comes from your loss of gravitational potential energy.

Have a friend hold your bicycle upright with the pedal in its highest position. **Put your helmet on.** When you are ready, stand upright with your entire weight on the pedal. Your weight will cause the pedal to turn to its lowest position. Try not to put any force on the handlebars as the pedal falls. If you have difficulty starting at the top position of the pedal, you may find it easier to start with the pedal in its horizontal position. You will fall only half as far, but you may find it easier to avoid pushing on the handlebars.

To see how much energy you transferred, you will need to measure the velocity of the bicycle after the pedal reaches its lowest position. If you have a bicycle with a speedometer, simply read the maximum speed after you have done the work on the bike. If you do not have a speedometer, you can measure the speed with a friend as you did in Experiment 12 when you measured speed with a stopwatch and a tape measure. Knowing the velocity and the mass of you and your bike, you can calculate the kinetic energy. Remember, one kilogram is equal to 2.2 pounds.

How much work did you do? How much kinetic energy was transferred to the bike and yourself? How efficiently did you transfer your gravitational potential energy to kinetic energy?

Science Project Ideas

- Do you think the results of Experiment 21 will be different if you have the bike in different gears? Try it! Was your prediction correct?
- Design and carry out an experiment to show that when a heavy object falls a short distance through air, the kinetic energy it gains is nearly equal to the gravitational potential energy it loses. Why is this not true for light objects such as paper or feathers?

Experiment 22

Doing Work and Generating Power in Different Gears

Materials

* multi-geared bicycle with a speedometer if possible

* **bicycle helmet**

* long, smooth, level path

* speedometer or a friend, a stopwatch, and a tape measure

* stopwatch or watch with a second hand or mode

* bathroom scale

* hat or piece of cloth

Wearing your bicycle helmet, start with a bicycle at rest on a smooth, level path. One pedal of the bike should be in its highest position. Now accelerate the bicycle by pushing on the pedals ten times in succession with as much force as you can muster. What is the bike's speed after you apply the final push?

If the bicycle has a speedometer, you can simply read the speed on the dial. If it is not equipped with a speedometer, you can measure the speed with a friend as you did in Experiment 12 by using a stopwatch and a tape measure.

Repeat the experiment in different gears. How do the final speeds compare? Can you explain why?

Repeat the experiment again in a number of different gears, but this time have a friend measure the time it takes to reach maximum speed in each gear. Is the time to reach maximum speed related to the gear the bike is in? If it is, can you explain why?

Power is the rate at which work or energy is generated.

That is,

$$power = \frac{energy\ (work\ done)}{time}$$

The metric unit used to measure power is the watt. (Can you guess for whom the unit of power was named?) One watt is equal to one joule per second or one newton-meter per second.

From the mass of you and your bicycle and the maximum speed you acquired in each timed experiment, you can determine the kinetic energy you obtained by doing work on the pedals. Using the time to achieve this energy, you can determine the power you developed. Does your power depend on the gear the bike is in?

One horsepower is equal to 746 watts. Were you able to work like a horse in any of the gears you used? How much horsepower did you develop in each case?

When you accelerate, your speed changes. Acceleration is defined as change in velocity divided by the time for that change to take place. That is,

$$acceleration = \frac{change\ in\ speed}{time}$$

When you exerted a force on your bicycle by pressing down hard on the pedals ten times in succession, your bike accelerated from rest (speed = 0) to a final speed. To find your average acceleration, have a friend start a stopwatch at the moment you start to pedal. Hold a hat or a piece of cloth against the outside edge of one handlebar. When you reach top speed, release the hat or cloth and look at your speedometer. When your friend sees the hat or cloth begin to fall, she should stop the stopwatch. Given your top speed and the time your friend measured, how can you calculate your average acceleration? Why does this experiment measure *average* acceleration?

What is the acceleration of your bicycle when you ride at a steady speed?

Science Project Ideas

- Design and carry out an experiment to find the acceleration of your bicycle when you coast down a long hill. Is the acceleration constant? Remembering Newton's second law of motion, how can you determine the net force acting on the bicycle as it rolls down the hill?
- Design and carry out an experiment to determine your average acceleration without using a speedometer.
    - Determine your bike's average acceleration (or deceleration, if it is slowing down) when you coast from a certain speed until you stop. Then determine your bike's average acceleration when you brake from a certain speed to a stop.

By now you realize that there are many experiments you can do with bicycles. In this book you have done a few of them, but there are many more you could do. You have probably thought of some as you worked on the ones described here. That is the way science works—one experiment leads to another. If you have enjoyed experimenting with bicycles, continue to do experiments that you design yourself. Who knows, you might use one as a project for your next science fair!

Glossary

acceleration—A change in velocity over time.

axle—The shaft on which a wheel turns.

ball bearing—A sphere, usually made of steel, that is used to reduce friction.

brake—A device designed to decrease the speed of a vehicle.

brake levers—Levers mounted on the handlebars that control the brakes.

centrifuge—A device designed to separate materials of different density by spinning them in a circular path at high speed.

chain—A series of joined links used to connect the gear or gears of the front sprocket of a bicycle with the gear or gears of the rear sprocket.

circumference—The perimeter of a circle, which is equal to the diameter of a circle times pi (π).

coaster brake—A brake mechanism that acts on the rear axle. It is activated by pushing backward on the pedals.

cranks—The shafts that connect the front sprocket with the pedals.

derailleur—A device that moves the chain from one gear to another on either sprocket.

differential gear—A gearing device that allows two wheels connected to the same axle to turn at different speeds.

efficiency—The ratio of work output to work input.

force—A push or a pull that can cause a body to accelerate.

fork—The two-pronged device that connects the front wheel to the frame of a bicycle.

friction—The force that resists the motion of one body relative to another.

gear-inches—In bicycles,

$$\text{gear-inches} = \frac{\text{number of teeth on front sprocket gear}}{\text{number of teeth on rear sprocket gear}} \times \text{wheel diameter (in inches)}$$

gears—Toothed wheels that intermesh either directly or by means of a chain.

gravity—The force of attraction between two masses. The force is proportional to the masses of the two bodies and inversely proportional to the square of the distance between their centers.

hand brake—A lever connected to the handlebar, which, when squeezed, pulls a wire that forces a rubber pad against the rim of the bicycle's wheel. The frictional force reduces the wheel's speed. There are two hand brakes, one for each wheel.

handlebar—The curved metal steering bar that connects to the fork leading to the front wheel.

hub—The front and rear units that contain the axle and to which the wheel's spokes are attached.

kinetic energy—The energy of motion. For any mass m with a velocity v, its kinetic energy is equal to $1/2\ mv^2$.

machine—A device that changes the size or direction (or both) of a force applied to a body. Simple machines include the lever, wedge, inclined plane, pulley, screw, and wheel and axle.

mass—The amount of matter in a body. Mass is measured in kilograms (metric) or slugs (U.S. conventional).

mechanical advantage (MA)—The ratio of the output force to the input force.

Newton's laws of motion—The three laws that describe motion in terms of force, mass, and acceleration. First law: A body at rest or in motion maintains its state of motion unless acted upon by an outside force. Second law: When a net force acts on a body, that body accelerates in the direction of the net force; the acceleration of the body is proportional to the force and inversely proportional to the mass of the body. Third law: To every action force there is an equal but opposed reaction force, or the mutual reactions of two bodies upon one another are always equal in magnitude but oppositely directed.

pi (π)—The ratio of the circumference of a circle to its diameter, which is approximately 3.14.

potential energy—Stored energy that can do work. For example, a body that can fall from a height possesses gravitational potential energy because it can do work as it falls.

power—The rate of doing work. Power is measured in watts (joules/second).

speed—The distance traveled divided by the time (duration) of travel.

sprocket—A toothed wheel over which a chain moves. The front sprocket on a bicycle is turned by the pedals. The rear sprocket is connected to the rear wheel. The two sprockets are connected by a chain.

square root—A number which when multiplied by itself produces the given number. For example, the square root of 16 is 4, because $4 \times 4 = 16$.

strut—A bar or rod used to strengthen a framework.

velocity—Speed in a particular direction.

weight—The force with which gravity attracts a mass. Weight is measured in newtons (metric) or pounds (U.S. conventional).

wheels—The circular rotating parts on which a bicycle rolls.

work—The product of a force and the distance through which it acts. Work is measured in newton-meters or joules.

Further Reading

Bombaugh, Ruth. *Science Fair Success, Revised and Expanded.* Springfield, N.J.: Enslow Publishers, Inc., 1999.

Fleisher, Paul. *Objects in Motion: Principles of Classical Mechanics.* Minneapolis: Lerner Publications, 2002.

Gardner, Robert. *Science Fair Projects—Planning, Presenting, Succeeding.* Springfield, N.J.: Enslow Publishers, Inc., 1998.

Goodstein, Madeline. *Science Fair Success Using Newton's Laws of Motion.* Berkeley Heights, N.J.: Enslow Publishers, Inc., 2002.

Gutman, Bill. *Bicycling,* Mankato, Minn.: Capstone Press, 1995.

Haduch, Bill. *Go Fly a Bike!: The Ultimate Book About Bicycle Fun, Freedom & Science.* New York: Dutton Books, 2004.

Hautzig, David. *Pedal Power: How a Mountain Bike Is Made.* New York: Dutton Children's Books, 1996.

Internet Addresses

The Bicycle Museum of America.
  http://www.bicyclemuseum.com

Pedaling History Bicycle Museum.
  "There's More to Bicycles Than You Think."
  http://www.pedalinghistory.com

The Ultimate Science Fair Resource.
  http://www.scifair.org

Index